Survival Guide to Confirmation

The Candidate's Guide

by
Dr Stephen Gomez

Reflections by
Fr Mossie Lyons OMI

Drawings by
Julian Quaye

Cover by Nick Park

ST PAULS

To the programme director

■ This book is the *Candidate's Guide* and it contains the learning material for use with the candidates. The *Catechist's Guide* is a separate book containing the candidate's material together with background explanatory notes.

■ This programme has developed over a decade of preparing Confirmation candidates and the lessons presented here have been well tried and tested.

■ Each catechist should possess a *Catechist's Guide* and each candidate a *Candidate's Guide*. Please refrain from photocopying the material because if you do we cannot cover costs.

———————————

Acknowledgements

I am most grateful to Bishop Mervyn Alexander Diocese of Clifton, Deacon Dennis Sutton, Director of Religious Education at the Clifton Religious Centre, and Sr Margaret Crowley SMG for helpful comments on the manuscript. I am also indebted to numerous catechists and candidates over the years. The programme is dedicated to my parents Stella & Len Gomez to whom I owe my faith.

Copyright © ST PAULS 1993

The Scripture quotations in this publication are from the New Jerusalem Bible © 1985 by Darton Longman & Todd Ltd and Doubleday & Company. Inc. and are used by permission.

ST PAULS Publishing
187 Battersea Bridge Road
London SW11 3AS, UK

Third Revised Edition 2000

ISBN 085439 437 0

Set by TuKan DTP, Fareham, UK
Produced in the EU
Printed in Malta by Melita Press

ST PAULS is an activity of the priests and brothers of the Society of St Paul
who proclaim the Gospel through the media of social communication

Contents

1. Knowing Me – Knowing You

Yo!

What's your handle?

Share & share alike

Welcome to this first Confirmation session and thanks for taking the time and effort to come along.

Before we get going, there may be some people in the group that you don't know. The first step in getting to know people is to greet them. There are many ways of greeting people in a friendly manner. You can say: hi, hello, watcha, alright then? Yo dude, Eh up, or shake their hand.

Remembering the names of people you've been introduced to can be difficult. This is one way to help you.

■ Sit in a circle – making sure you're sitting next to someone you don't know.

■ ... wait

■ Form pairs with your neighbour.

■ Each pair faces one another and has 4 minutes (2 mins each) to find out as much about the other person's name as possible. Ask what their name is, does he/she like his/her name, who was he/she named after, does he/she

When the others in the group were being introduced you might have noticed that there were things that you shared with them. For instance, the same age, school, number of sisters/brothers. Although everyone is unique there are many things we share.

To find out just what we have in common complete the following survey. In the table on the facing

What other greetings have you come across or use?

Very soon we are going to find out who's who in the group and when you come across someone that you don't know make sure you greet him or her and tell them your name.

have a nickname or a shortened name, is there a special spelling of their name etc.

■ At the end of the 4 minutes you have to introduce the person you were interviewing to the rest of the group by repeating what you were told about their name. This is a good memory test to see how much you remember.

■ This time, form new pairs and repeat the interviewing technique but now ask each other about their families, school, likes and dislikes etc. Then get into the large group and share what you have discovered.

page fill in your details in the first column. Then you have 5 minutes to go around as many members of the group as you can and find out what they have in common with you. If you share a point tick the box or put a cross if they differ.

You	other people				
	1	2	3	4	5
Name	❑	❑	❑	❑	❑
Age	❑	❑	❑	❑	❑
Where born	❑	❑	❑	❑	❑
Hair colour	❑	❑	❑	❑	❑
Eye colour	❑	❑	❑	❑	❑
No. brothers	❑	❑	❑	❑	❑
No. sisters	❑	❑	❑	❑	❑
Shoe size	❑	❑	❑	❑	❑
Favourite pop singer	❑	❑	❑	❑	❑
Squeeze toothpaste from the middle Yes	❑	❑	❑	❑	❑

One thing you probably share with the others in the group is a fear of what is going to happen in these sessions. It is said that one way of overcoming your fears is to face them. What are your fears and expectations? Tick the thoughts which come closest to yours at this moment:

❑ 'I hope these lessons aren't going to be boring. I hate RE classes.'

❑ 'don't want to be here. My parents forced me to come along.'

❑ 'Everyone says it's time to make my Confirmation, so that's why I'm here."

❑ 'I wonder what Confirmation is all about. How's it going to help me be a good Catholic? I'd like to find out more.'

❑ 'I hope it's not all praying and religious stuff like that.'

❑ 'I don't know much about religion, I hope I'm not asked a lot of questions."

❑ 'I've had a hard day at school, and this is the last place I want to be. I wish I was at home watching TV.'

In these sessions, you will spend some time learning and some time praying, some time discussing and doing activities. Above all it's hoped that you'll spend a lot of time enjoying yourself – so you shouldn't have anything to fear.

No fear!

Your thoughts?

2. So You Want To Be Confirmed?

Why do you want to be confirmed?

Seven things you could be doing if you weren't here:
- ◆ watching TV
- ■ playing football
- ● doing homework
- ▼ having piano lessons
- ◆ roaming the street
- ▲ doing the washing up
- ■ playing computer games

What else could you be doing?

_____

_____

_____

_____

Many candidates attend Confirmation classes because they have been forced to do so by their mother, father, grandparents or other relatives. Who in their right mind would want to attend religion classes when they could be doing something else?

Well, there are some very good reasons for being confirmed and during the preparation you'll discover some of them.

Confirmation involves taking more responsibility for your own religious life and the best time to start practising this is now. For you to gain anything from these sessions it is important that you choose to attend freely of your own will.

Choice is an important part of life and people will respect your decision of whether you proceed with the preparation or not.

What am I missing on TV tonight by being here?

What is Confirmation?

What do you think Confirmation means or represents?

Write down your understanding of Confirmation, then share your answers with the group.

_____

_____

_____

Confirmation has different meanings to different people, for example:

- ■ it's a confirming of what was done on your behalf at Baptism
- ■ it's a celebration that marks the ending of the process of Christian initiation begun at Baptism
- ■ it's a sense of belonging to the Christian community
- ■ it's a ceremony whereby candidates receive the gifts of the Holy Spirit in a special way
- ■ it provides a setting for a deeper understanding of Christ
- ■ it's a process in which the candidates are made more aware of Christ working in their lives and through the lives of others around them

Confirmation isn't any one of these – but all of them!

Have you got street cred?
Do you...

☐ buy the latest in trainers and sports wear?
☐ keep up with the latest music?
☐ buy video games?
☐ long for/buy the latest fashions?
☐ treat the opposite sex as 'sex objects'?

If your answer is yes to all of these – you have serious cred!

Now try these. Do you...

☐ admit to being a Christian?
☐ feel sorry for those in need?
☐ want to live a good and honest life?
☐ care about your family?
☐ like helping people?

If your answer is yes to all of these – you have serious cred problems!

Life is geared for the young. If you walk down any high street you'll see:

■ record shops selling the latest CDs and singles that you must buy
■ advertising posters proclaiming the latest films and fashions
■ sports/clothes shops displaying the latest fashions.

If you want to be in fashion and have street cred and keep in with other young people then you have to keep up appearances and know what's happening in music.

All the latest fashions for the young are called youth culture.

Who decides:

▼ what should be youth culture?
▲ what is in and out of fashion?

Big business such as record, sports and fashion companies have a vested interest in keeping products going in and out of fashion. A new pair of trainers comes into fashion, you buy them, and before you've worn them out, there's a new model which you have to buy, and so on. The message is – *You can only have fun if you have money!*

Life is constantly on the move and ever changing. If it stayed still you would probably get bored.

Write down your last three favourite groups/singers and for roughly how long each was your favourite?

Do the same for your favourite films, trainers, tracksuits, hair-styles etc.

Find out from your parents their answers to the same questions when they were your age.

When you constantly spend money to buy into a culture it is looked upon as *consumerism* or *materialism*. This is where big business wins out. Just as CDs are replacing LPs, hi-fi companies will bring out yet another format for you to spend your money on.

Does consumerism bring happiness ?

The answer is, in the short term, it can. That computer game that you desperately wanted and couldn't live without – you eventually became tired of it. The trouble with materialism is that – you want it, you have it, and you soon become bored by it. To keep happy you have to buy something else... and so on.

Life moves so fast that you just have time to experience things but not think about anything or reflect on it for any length of time. If you did you might see its unimportance. Is there a way out of this situation? The answer from a Christian point of view is very much yes. A Christian need not shun material goods. They don't have to live in a cave. They can still buy cars, hi-fi, fashionable clothes – but these things are not the most important things in life. They are not the sole reason for happiness but improve the quality of life.

To a Christian there is something more important that does bring happiness to his or her life. That something is knowledge and acceptance of Jesus working in their life. This may not seem all that exciting news. Until, that is, you experience Jesus working in your life.

◆ Jesus is constant and stable
◆ we change but Jesus doesn't
◆ He is always with us, helping us if we allow Him to
◆ Jesus allows us to live life to the full and offers an alternative to finding happiness only in material goods.

3. Me, Myself, I

Unique & gifted

Young people sometimes have a bad name! Older people often complain that the young are:

○ too noisy
○ rude to elders
○ a lazy bunch of layabouts
○ self-centred, only think about themselves
○ never up to any good
○ unappreciative
○ always wanting money to go out
○ wanting expensive designer clothes

How true are these statements about you?

The sort of people who would make these comments would be surprised to know that all young people (as does everyone) have gifts and talents.

If you were asked what gifts or talents you have, you might be too embarrassed to say. Being brought up not to brag, we leave it to others to recognise our talents. It's important to recognise your own gifts, because you will then be in a better position to offer them to others. Your gifts and talents are given by God and it's up to you to use and develop them.

The good, the bad and the ugly

In some ways we can be likened to a rose bush! A rose bush is planted deeply in the soil and draws nourishment through its roots. Its stem is strong and gives it support and at the end of its branches are some unopened rose buds and some fully opened roses. The picture of the rose bush represents you.

Write by the:

■ **roots** – the people and things that nourish and feed your character

■ **stem** – personal gifts and talents that strengthen you

■ **open roses** – talents already used to help the people in your life

■ **unopened buds** – talents you haven't offered or used yet

■ **thorns** – the less good things about you that stop people coming close to you or put people off.

Being part of a society means having to meet and deal with people. Some people you enjoy being with and have as close friends. Others you might dislike and not want to be with. You don't know the majority of people in society, so you probably have no feelings about them one way or the other. Because they are still part of your community you might come across some of them at some point. How should we treat other people?

Read the accounts about Sebastian written by Richard, a classmate, and by his social worker, Mr Williams.

Sebastian by Richard

Sebastian joined my class late in the year. No one likes him. He looks funny, because he has a red mark on the side of his face. It's only a small mark but you can't help noticing it. He doesn't take part in any sports or anything. Whenever you talk to him he's not friendly at all, and doesn't say much. He never invites anyone back to his house and he's never about to play after school or at weekends. If the teacher asks him to do anything like read aloud, he's rude and starts messing about. He's just a loner.

Does Sebastian appeal to you as someone you'd like to befriend? Everyone is against Sebastian; would that influence your opinion of him?

Sebastian by Mr Williams

I have been Sebastian's social worker since soon after he was born. As a baby, he was physically abused by his parents and was admitted into hospital after being scalded badly by boiling water thrown at him. He has terrible scars on his body that will never disappear, but luckily only part of the scars shows when he is clothed, a small mark on his face. He was removed from his parents and placed in a children's home. The terrible events he has experienced have naturally affected his education and it seems that he suffers from dyslexia. Considering what he has gone through, he has emerged a wonderful person and he wanted to attend the local school instead of a special school. Sebastian wants and needs to be loved and befriended.

Does Sebastian appeal to you as someone you'd like to befriend knowing his background?

Other people's history

To get the right answer you must ask the right question. At the start of the programme you got to know the other people in the class by comparing your features, such as hair colour etc with theirs. Is this the best way to get to know what a person is really like ? If you were to interview them now what questions would you ask ? Write down a list of questions you'd need to ask about a person to know them properly.

_____

_____

_____

_____

Guess the person

Name of person:

Five clues about them (starting with a hard clue and becoming easier)

1.

2.

3.

4.

5.

4. Do You Wanna Be in My Gang?

Come & join us

If you were asked to join a group or club that you knew nothing about, would you say yes or no? It is very likely that you'll say 'It depends'. Before making up your mind you would need to know about the people in the group, what they are like, their interests and what they do.

A group is only as good as its members – so you have to ask yourself what you can offer the others in the group.

Are you a member of a club or group already?

If so, what sort of people make up the group, what are they like and what do they do?

What are the qualities of a good group member?

What's a community?

The members of a gang or a group usually have something in common. A group of people who form a football team, are obviously all interested in playing football. The members of a fan club of a pop star have in common the music of that pop singer.

Everyone belongs to a group called the community. You belong to a local community in the area where you live and for your local community to work properly everyone has a responsibility.

Your neighbourhood is run by the Council.

What does your local Council supply you with?

What jobs are needed to be done to keep your local community working?

What responsibility do you have to your local community?

A community may also share certain beliefs in common. The Christian community for instance shares the same belief – that is, following the teachings of Jesus Christ.

You were made part of the Christian community at your Baptism. If you were baptised as a baby you obviously didn't have a choice in the matter. Your parents and god-parents put you forward and took baptismal promises on your behalf. At the time it was understood that you were going to be brought up in the Catholic faith and when you were old enough

you would take these baptismal promises yourself.

Part of the Confirmation ceremony will involve you confirming these baptismal promises and, by so doing, you will be declaring that you have decided to be a member of the Church – rather than your parents deciding for you.

Should you be confirmed or shouldn't you? Only you can truthfully decide. If you are unsure at present then that is fine because you probably need to know more before making your mind up.

Do you like making decisions? Or do you like other people deciding for you?

When you were a baby there were very few decisions that you could make for yourself. You were dependent upon your parents or guardians to look after you. As you grow older you will take more and more responsibility for your own life. Part of becoming more responsible is making decisions yourself.

Who decided that you should be baptised? Who decided that you should receive your First Holy Communion? Who should decide that you should make your Confirmation?

For each of the following stages in life, make a list of the things that you decide or decided and that your parents decide or decided for you.

◆ infancy
◆ primary school
◆ early secondary school
◆ now

	Decisions made by me	Decisions made by parents
Infancy		
Primary school		
Early secondary school		
Now		

**Activity: Choices –
The Computer Game
of Life**

5. The God Squad

Catechists have to make decisions. At the Confirmation Mass the Bishop will ask the catechists if they think you are ready to be Confirmed. If a catechist says 'yes' he or she will have to mean it. People like you who are being prepared for Confirmation are called candidates.

You must have heard this term used when people are up for election.

Election candidates put themselves forward for consideration – they do not have an automatic right to be an MP – they must show themselves worthy. That is why they are referred to as candidates. You also have to show that you are worthy and up to the task of taking on the responsibilities that Confirmation will confer on you.

What is Church?

	Your opinion	Church's opinion
pollution/ environment		
nuclear war		
relationships		
violence/crime		
handicapped		
racism		
starvation		
poverty		
feminism		

If you were asked to explain the word 'church', you might say it's a building where people pray. This is partly true as you can still have a Church without any buildings! This is because the Church is made up of people called the 'congregation' or the 'faithful'.

A lot of people, especially the young, think that the idea of the Church is old fashioned and has nothing to contribute to our modern society. This is far from the truth. The table lists some current issues about our modern society. In the first column write down what you think about these issues, then in the second column write down what you think the Church says about the same issues. Feel free to include other current issues.

As we saw earlier, to get to know someone well, you need to spend time with them. To get to know what Confirmation means and the importance of Christ working in your life, you need to spend time too. This programme can be thought of as a journey along which you may gain a better understanding of Confirmation and the implications of being a confirmed Christian. Our companions on this journey are the others in the class. Like any other journey we can have a better time if we share with others along the way.

We saw earlier that your Council looks after the area where you live. Your local Christian community, however, is based around your local parish. Try to answer the questions below about your parish.

Who runs your parish?

What jobs are needed to be done in the parish to keep it 'alive'?

Are ordinary people needed to keep their parish community working properly, if so how can they help?

What groups are there in your local parish?

What do you understand by a 'God squad'? Who might they be? What might they do? How could they carry out their mission?

6. Once a Catholic

'Once a Catholic, always a Catholic' as the saying goes. But what is a Catholic? Most people would answer 'a Catholic goes to Mass and Confession, and they're against abortion and birth control'.

Here's a list of activities, not in any particular order, which is often associated with being a Catholic:

❑ going to Mass every Sunday

❑ reading and knowing the Bible

❑ eating fish on a Friday

❑ praying

❑ loving and caring for everyone

❑ going to Confession

❑ against abortion and contraception

Put these statements in your order of importance by writing a number in each of the boxes. 1 is very important, 7 least important. Explain your reasons.

Can you think of any other activities associated with Catholics?

The Creed

What a Catholic should believe in is summed up in the Creed – a prayer usually said during the Mass. Read through the Creed then answer the questions below.

We believe in one God
the Father, the Almighty,
maker of heaven and earth,
of all that is, seen and unseen.
We believe in one Lord,
   Jesus Christ,
the only Son of God,
eternally begotten of the Father,
God from God, Light from Light,
true God from true God,
begotten, not made,
of one being with the Father.
Through him all things were
   made.
For us men and for our salvation
he came down from heaven:
by the power of the Holy Spirit

he became incarnate from the
   Virgin Mary, and was made
   man.
For our sake he was crucified
   under Pontius Pilate;
he suffered death and was
   buried.
On the third day he rose again
in accordance with the
   Scriptures;
he ascended into heaven
and is seated at the right hand
   of the Father.
He will come again in glory to
   judge the living and the dead,
and his kingdom will have no
   end.

We believe in the Holy Spirit,
   the Lord, the giver of life,
who proceeds from the Father
   and the Son.
With the Father and the Son he
   is worshipped and glorified.
He has spoken through the
   Prophets.
We believe in one, holy, catholic,
   and apostolic Church.
We acknowledge one baptism for
   the forgiveness of sins.
We look for the resurrection of
   the dead,
and thelife of the world to come.
   Amen.

Creed quiz

Cover up the Creed given above and try to answer these questions.

How many times do we say 'we believe'?

Name three things we believe about God the Father.

Name five things we believe about God the Son.

Name three things we believe about God the Holy Spirit.

Who was Pontius Pilate?

Name some Prophets the Holy Spirit has spoken through.

What is meant by 'life of the world to come'?

Try writing out your personal creed, that is the things you believe in and find important in life. To give you an idea, this is a creed written by a group of six young lads:

We believe in one God,
We believe that Jesus Christ lived as a man.
We believe that he was God's Son and that he died and rose for us.
We believe that he redeemed us from our sins.
We believe in life for our eternal souls.
We believe that we are blinded by temptation and that we must look to the light of Christ for guidance.
We believe in the Bible's teachings.

We believe in the Holy Spirit by whom we are to be Confirmed.
We believe that we should love.
We believe that we should look upon each other as equals.
We believe in freedom of choice.
We believe in free speech.
We believe in fulfilment in life.
We believe in enjoying that life.
We believe in honesty.
We believe in prayer.

I believe...

_____

_____

_____

_____

_____

_____

_____

_____

Church history and the Mass

Each of us has a 'milestone' in our life, such as a birthday or wedding anniversary which is celebrated every year.

The Church has a number of milestones which are celebrated on certain dates. Some of these events occur on the same date every year and some, called movable feasts, occur on slightly different dates from one year to another. These special occasions are celebrated in the setting of the Mass. There are so many important events that the Mass emphasises different aspects at different parts of the year. Below is a selection of remembered special occasions. For each of the events below, find out the date when it is celebrated and the meaning behind the celebration.

	Date	Meaning
Advent		
Immaculate Conception		
Christmas Day		
Epiphany		
Baptism of Our Lord		
Ash Wednesday		
Palm Sunday		
Good Friday		
Easter Sunday		
Ascension		
Pentecost		
Corpus Christi		
Assumption		
All Saints' Day		
All Souls' Day		

7. I Have Good News...

'I have good news... and I have bad news.' How many jokes have you heard starting like that? News, either personal or national, forms an important part of our lives.

Who were the people who made the news during this week?

Here are names of people who made the news in the past: Princess Diana, Mother Teresa, Charles Darwin, Nelson Mandela. Have you heard of any of them? If so, can you remember why they made the news?

People become newsworthy for different reasons. They may be leaders, heroes, sports people, film stars, pop stars and scientists. Each was an important person at the time they made the news. But life moves on – leaders change, there are new and different kinds of music, new records are achieved in sports, and in science new discoveries are made.

Newsmakers of the past are remembered but their lives and personalities don't affect us that much and their influence and achievements fade or are superseded by progress or refinements.

Jesus the newsmaker

One person in history still commands incredible respect, influence and attention. That person is Jesus Christ. Why? Because no other person has affected, and still affects, the course of history as much as this one extraordinary man.

Think of Jesus' influence in just one small area of life and expression – the arts. In recent times musicians, artists and film-makers have tried to portray His life and what He stands for. Each new generation tries to unearth a new facet or understanding of His life and personality.

Some films include: Jesus of Nazareth, The Life of Brian, Jesus Christ Superstar, The Last Temptation.

Can you name others?

Who is Jesus?

If someone who knew nothing about Jesus asked you about Him and the sort of person He is, what would you say, or where would you direct him/her to find out?

■ Plan out a course of study for them.

You can tell what people are like by knowing:
> who they go around with,
> how they treat people,
> how they talk to people,
> how they behave.

The Gospels tell us what Jesus was like by recording who He went around with, how He treated people, what He said to them and how He behaved.

The Jerusalem Chronicle

This is one way of investigating what Jesus is like. Your Confirmation group is going to act as investigative reporters working for the newspaper *The Jerusalem Chronicle*. You are all gathered together in the Editor's office awaiting your briefing for the assignment. Each person needs a Bible.

Editor: Thank you all for coming along to this briefing session. I think we have a really big story on our hands and I'm pulling you all out of your current assignments to work on this story for a special issue of the Chronicle.

The story is about a person called Jesus Christ who roamed around Palestine preaching and performing miracles. I know we've heard all this before – but this is the new angle – he claimed to be both **human** and **divine**, and people are beginning to believe this. He was executed a few weeks ago and some people say he's come back from the dead.

I want you to find out as much about this Jesus Christ as you can. I've compiled a list of people for you to interview from different times in his life. If you can't find out all the facts fill in the details yourself.

Write your reports and make it interesting for the readers. Compose a headline as well. We'll meet back here for you to read your articles. Remember the angle – **human** and **divine**. Decide for yourself which applies more in your story.

■ choose one or more of the following assignments
■ write out the assignments in the form of newspaper articles
■ make up a poster in newspaper form – with headlines and photographs'.

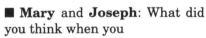

Editorial briefing list – Profile of Jesus Christ
people to be interviewed and example questions to ask

■ the **woman** who directed Mary and Joseph to the stable: Did you think the couple were special in any way? Why?

■ **Herod** (Mt 2:13-18): Why did you feel threatened?

■ **Mary** and **Joseph** (Lk 1:26-38; Mt 1:18-25): How did you know that baby Jesus was special?

■ **shepherds** (Lk 2:8-20): Why do you think you were chosen to be present after the birth?

■ **three wise men** (Mt 2:1-12): What made you come all this way?

■ **Simeon** (Lk 2:25-35): Why were you waiting all these years?

Jesus – as a baby

■ **Mary** and **Joseph**: What did you think when you
• first discovered He was missing
• when you found Him in the temple
• when He explained why He went missing (Lk 2:41-50)

Jesus – as a young boy of 12 years

■ (Lk 2:51-52): What was Jesus doing when He was a young man, before starting His public work?

Jesus – as a young man

Jesus – in His public ministry

■ the **Samaritan woman** at the well: Jesus had a profound impact upon you, why was this? (Jn 4: 5-26)

■ the **trader** in the temple market place: Jesus upset your stall, did He have any reason to act like this? (Jn 2:13-17)

■ **Peter**: You knew Jesus very well. Did you actually see Him perform any miracle? (Jairus' daughter); Who do you say He really was? How did He treat people? Did He wash your feet? (Jn 13:6-11)

■ the **other disciples**: What was Jesus' mood in the Garden of Gethsemane? (Mk 14:32-42)

■ the **followers** waiting near the cross: What did you hear Jesus say on the cross? (Mt 27:45-50)

■ the **centurion** who scourged Jesus: You were following orders, but how did you feel about inflicting pain? (Jn 19:1-3)

■ **John**: Before Jesus died, what special favour did He ask?

■ **person** in the synagogue (Mt 5:17-19): Jesus made some astonishing claims about fulfilling the Scriptures, how did you feel about what He was saying?

■ **disciple** in the boat (Mt 8:23-27): You were there when Jesus calmed the storms, how did He do it? You also saw Him walking on water, did anyone else try? (Mt 14:22-33)

■ **James**: You were there when Jesus was transfigured, what were your feelings? (Mt 17:1-8)

■ **Mary Magdalene**: You claim Jesus appeared to you after His death. Can you explain what happened? (Mk 16:9-11)

Overall picture

What is the overall picture you have of Jesus? Write a few sentences of your view of Jesus. Has He something to say to us today? How and where can you see Him affecting the world today? Jesus is obviously more than just a newsmaker – but what?

_____

_____

_____

_____

Human and divine

Jesus was both human and divine. Why did God appear in 'human' form? People have been trying to answer this question for centuries. The answer might be that Jesus came to be an example to us, that is, people can relate more easily to another human being living a similar life and facing similar problems to us. The way Jesus reacted to our problems was appropriate to His divinity. That is, He was able to empathise with us, recognise our needs, and respond by healing and forgiving our sins. In this way Jesus came to redeem us, that is to save us from sin and show the way to God the Father. Jesus also came to show us what God is like, that is – He is the revelation of God. We are expected to emulate Jesus, which means to live our lives by recognising the needs of others and trying to help them.

In your life you'll get to know certain people better than others. Some of these people are very special to you.

Which people in your life are special to you?

_____

What makes them special?

_____

How do you treat special people?

_____

You probably spend a lot of time with people you find special. You want to be with them and get to know them well. By spending time with them you form a relationship.

Jesus is a very special person, especially to Christians. It is worth spending time and forming a relationship with Him because He is special.

In what ways can you spend time with Jesus?

_____

Read the story of Jesus and the miracle of the loaves (Mt 15: 32-39).

Imagine that you are one of the people in the crowd.

Draw out a picture of Jesus and look at the face.

As you're looking at Jesus looking at you, what is He saying to you?

Is He pleased?

What is He asking of you?

How could you apply His wishes to your everyday life?

8. A Sign of the Times

What is a sign?

Signs and symbols play an important part in the Church, especially for you at Confirmation. They are used to convey some very profound messages.

Signs have been used throughout history and their use continues even today. A sign points the way or gives information. Common examples of signs include: road signs, signs to distinguish between men's and women's toilets, shop signs.

Other less obvious signs include: marks you receive for exams and homework, for example A- or D+; these signs provide a convenient way of letting you know how well you performed. There are facial signs – made by contracting the muscles in our face. We communicate with others through facial expressions; smiling, frowning or crying can be expressed more simply through facial expressions than explaining these feelings verbally.

Can you think of other examples of everyday signs?

Make a list of some signs you have encountered and explain their underlying meaning.

Make up a sign of your own and see if the others in the group can guess its message.

Symbols embody a deeper and less obvious meaning. Common examples include: a national flag and company logos, school crest, coat of arms and the Olympic rings. If you saw a BT or Nike logo you'd understand what was being offered – but someone not knowing that these represented company products would be baffled.

Your sign

What use are signs?

Signs are used to communicate, in simple terms, a complicated idea so that the majority of people can understand its meaning.

Hundreds of years ago, many people could not read, and signs were used widely for communication between people. Shops had signs outside with images of what was on sale inside, so the fishmongers had a fish sign hanging outside the shop and the baker had a sign of a loaf of bread, etc. When illiterate people signed a document they could not write their name so instead they signed their name with a cross.

Signs have to be public; if they were hidden 'inside' they would be of no use in communicating or publicising their message.

The Church's signs

Many signs are used in the Church; these signs, called Sacraments, use symbols to communicate something deeper. A Sacrament is a sign of what God is doing in our lives. The greatest sign of God's love for us is His Son Jesus.

Jesus Christ came to Earth as a sign from God that He loves us (Jn 3:17). Because of our human weakness and tendency to turn away from God's invitation to love, Jesus came to offer us forgiveness and to draw us closer to His Father. Jesus' death on the Cross and His resurrection are the greatest signs of how much God loves us and wishes to share with us in life that has no end.

Through His life on earth, Jesus showed us what God is like. In Jesus, we see God as a caring and loving person. When we see Jesus with people like the blind man, the tax collectors and sinners (such as the woman caught up in adultery) we come to understand the meaning of genuine love, compassion and forgiveness.

God the Father

God the Father has been depicted throughout our history in various ways. A common picture of God the Father that many people have is as an old man with a white beard!

What is your image of God the Father?

God the Son, Jesus Christ

God the Son is also represented in many ways. He is presented as a man in the person of Jesus Christ; as the alpha (α) and the omega (Ω), the first and the last, the beginning and the end; as a bright light in the transfiguration, when some of His disciples saw Him as He really was; in the Mass He is represented by the appearances of bread and wine; we often think of Jesus as a shepherd, who cares and looks after His flock; and as a lamb, an animal that is very gentle but often used in sacrifices.

How do you see God the Son?

God the Holy Spirit

God the Holy Spirit is represented as wind blowing over the face of the waters in the formation of the world in the Book of Genesis; as a dove at Christ's baptism; as a gusting wind at Pentecost; as tongues of fire descending on the Apostles.

How would you represent God the Holy Spirit?

The Trinity

God the Father, Son, and Holy Spirit together make up the Trinity. The Sign of the Cross is a sign of both the Cross of Calvary and a reminder of the Trinity.

St Patrick used a shamrock to represent the Trinity. He said that although there are three separate leaves in a shamrock, they are, in fact, joined up by a single stem.

How would you represent the Trinity?

9. The Magnificent Seven

What is a friend?

What is a friend? A friend is a person who:
■ you know and who knows you well
■ you get on with and in whom you can confide
■ you have affection for
■ is loyal and supports you
■ accepts you for what you are
■ spends time with you

During your life, friends will come and friends will go. Even if you have a life-long friend it's likely there'll be times when you'll fall out. There is however one person who is literally your friend for life – that person is Jesus. Jesus has all the qualities listed, but differs from all other friends because He is *always* with you and willing to help.

A friend in Jesus

When Jesus was on earth, His followers regarded Him as their friend. Jesus cared for people and wanted to help them, not necessarily in material ways, but to lead them towards His Father in heaven. Imagine being alive in Jesus' time and having Him as a friend. Also, imagine what it must have been like when Jesus ascended into heaven. His followers were devastated at the thought of losing Him! But Jesus being a good and loyal friend wouldn't leave them in the lurch. He said He'd be with them always and promised to send them a helper to strengthen them.

In what way could Jesus always be with His followers?

Jesus is with you today

Although Jesus was on the earth over 2000 years ago He is working with us even today. His presence and power is celebrated in certain activities called Sacraments, which are: Baptism, Eucharist (or Holy Communion), Reconciliation (or Penance or Confession), Confirmation, Matrimony, Holy Orders, and Anointing of the Sick.

Each Sacrament is a celebration of Jesus' presence in our lives and His friendship with us and is accompanied by certain symbols and community ceremonies or celebrations. Ceremonies help celebrate the Sacrament in a consistent way.

Ceremonies form an important part of our lives and that of our society.

What ceremonies do you, your school and the nation perform?

The Sacraments are full of symbolism, involving everyday substances such as water, light, bread and wine. The meaning behind the use of such objects helps us come close to Jesus. As each Sacrament is discussed the symbols are explained. The first Sacrament, Baptism, is given below and the others are explored later.

Baptism

All friendships begin with an introduction. Baptism is the first Sacrament we experience and it is our introduction into God's family. If you were baptised as a baby you were, of course, not aware of this meeting with Jesus. However, from the moment you were born to this day Jesus knows you, loves and cares for you. As you have grown up you've got to know more and more about Jesus.

The origins of the symbols and ceremony of Baptism have roots which date far back in history. The word Baptism comes from the Greek meaning 'to bathe, dip or plunge in water'. In the Old Testament there are many references to ritual washing of the hands and feet before people entered the temple. This action was used to signify physical and spiritual 'cleansing' before entering somewhere sacred.

Many other religions also have a ritual washing, e.g. Muslims before entering the mosque and Hindus bathing in the sacred waters of the River Ganges. One of the earliest times we come across Baptism in the New Testament is when John is baptising people in God's name and he even baptises Jesus. Jesus' Baptism marked the beginning of His mission to carry out God's plan for humankind.

Baptism is rich in symbolism, using: water, lighted candle, a white gar-ment, and chrism (holy oil).

■ **water** has many uses. You need water to keep alive. In fact, about 70% of body weight is water. We wash and keep clean using water. The use of holy water in Baptism is a symbol of Christ keeping us alive spiritually.

■ **light** is a symbol often used in the Church. It is a sign that Christ is lighting your way and without Him you are in darkness and lost. Can you think of where or when candles are used in the Church?

■ **white garment**; in the early Church it was the custom that people preparing for Baptism wore sack-clothes and that during the ceremony of entering the Church on Easter Sunday they would take off their old clothes and put on a new white garment to symbolise a re-birth to a new life.

■ **oil** was used by athletes to increase the circulation to their skin and muscles to make them stronger. Oil was also used to anoint people when they became kings or leaders in order to strengthen them in their work. Oil is used in Baptism to strengthen the baptized in their faith in Christ. Oil of Catechumens is used for the first anointing and oil of Chrism for the second anointing.

How would you symbolise the meaning of Baptism?

10. Water & Fire
A Reflection on Baptism

God present through symbols

Sing the hymn: 'Be still' or 'As gentle as silence'.

Reading from the Bible: 1 Kings 19:9-14.

Symbol: Word of God

Reading: Heb 4:10-13 (The power of the word) or Is 55:10-11.

The Bible is incensed.

Baptismal background: Ephetha or touching of ears and mouth, praying that the child may soon listen to and proclaim the word of God.

Symbol: Water

Bowl of water is brought in and blessed.

Reading: Mt 28:18 or Mt 3:13-17.

The Creed is read – prayer of all the baptised and the profession of the faith.

Sprinkling (Sign of the Cross).

Hymn: 'Peace is flowing like a river'.

Baptismal background: Water gives life and allows for growth. God's family is initiated into the life of the Church in Baptism.

Symbol: Candle

Reading: Is 9:1-3 or Mt 5:14-16.

A large candle is incensed (the priest explains why).

Smaller candles are lit, one for each candidate; a candle was lit for you at your Baptism. You now voluntarily decide to witness to the light of Christ in our lives in word and by deeds.

Having lit small candles, pause for short silent prayer of self-recommitment to Christ.

The priest reads: Many people have kept the flame of faith burning brightly throughout the world, down through the centuries. They bore witness to Christ, our Light, through their self-giving in service of Him – a service of thought, word and deed. Service of God has involved suffering for many; sometimes even death. Today men and women continue to bear witness to the Light. Now we remember them and thank God for the example of their lives to us as Christians.

A candle is lit for each of the following (think of who these people are):

1. for those who suffer for their faith

2. for those who work for peace and justice

3. for the innocent victims of violence

4. for those who lead us with courage in the faith

God present through people

Christ is ever present in the Blessed Sacrament

Exposition of the Blessed Sacrament

Period of silence

Reading: Jn 6

Sign of Peace

God present through the Eucharist

11. What Should I Do?

Values

Earlier in the programme you looked at making decisions about your life. Some decisions you make will affect other people. The sort of decision you make depends on your values. What do you understand by the term 'value'? Many people would say how much it cost. There is a great difference between **cost** and **value**. Cost is the monetary price paid for something. Value is the desirability or importance of something to you. Values are the moral principles and beliefs, or standards of a person. A person's values determine what sort of person they are and how they treat other people and how they react to moral situations. The way you react to situations is called your behaviour.

Where does a person get his/her values from?

What influences a person's values?

Values of Jesus

If you know a person's values you can tell how that person will react to a situation. Jesus never made up lots of rules and regulations of things we can or cannnot do.

Instead, He revealed His values to us by the way in which He treated and spoke to people as recorded in the Bible.

By knowing Jesus' values, you can predict what Jesus would do in difficult situations, and therefore what we should do as well.

What do you think are the values of Jesus?

Values of other people

People have different values or standards. You may agree with some of their values but not others.

List 5 things about people's values that you don't like and that you do like.

_____
_____
_____
_____
_____

List 5 things about your values that you don't like and that you do like.

_____
_____
_____
_____
_____

Sinking boat

Imagine that everyone in your class is in a life-boat after the ship you've been travelling on sinks. There isn't enough room or food for all of you to survive.

Two people have to be thrown overboard to allow everyone else to survive. Each person states his/her values to the group and then you decide as a group what is to be done!

In life you are often called upon to make some difficult decisions. Read through the moral dilemmas in the next section. For each dilemma answer the following questions:

- what *would* you do?
- what *should* you do?
- what would *Jesus* do?

1. The examination

You are in the middle of an examination and finding it hard going. You haven't done much work for the exam but you need to pass. You are sitting next to the 'brain' of the class and you can see his answers without being noticed. Do you cheat?

2. Shoplifting

You are out shopping in a departmental store one day when you notice a girl from your class putting some perfume into her bag without paying for it.
Do you tell one of the shop assistants?

3. Stolen goods

Someone offers you a new bicycle at a low price that you can't refuse. But you know that it is probably stolen.
Do you buy it?

6. Marriage Problems

Sam and Geraldine went to a marriage counsellor to sort out their problems. 'I can't cope anymore' said Geraldine, 'Sam goes out for football training on Monday nights, and goes for a few drinks afterwards. He works late most Wednesdays and he's in the pub on Friday and Saturday, then there's usually a match on Sunday. I'm always alone with the children and he doesn't leave me much money to budget the bills.'
'That's not fair', said Sam. 'You knew that I liked to socialise when you married me. Besides I work hard all day, and I need to get away and relax in the evenings.'
What advice would you give to help Sam and Geraldine sort out their problems?

4. Save the whale

You are an active campaigner against the hunting and killing of whales. You attend rallies, write to your MP and join Greenpeace. At one of the rallies you feel ill. When you see your doctor he refers you to the hospital. After many tests you are found to have a rare disorder. Over many months of treatment it is found to be incurable. A friend reads in a newspaper that a Japanese doctor claims to have a cure for the disease – but one of the ingredients is a substance obtained from whales. Would you take the cure?

5. Parked car

You're driving at night. When going around a corner you accidentally scrape a parked car. No one saw you do it.
Do you stop and put a note on the car giving your name and address so the owner can claim off you?

8. An offer you can't refuse?

You and a friend have just had a holiday of a lifetime in the Far East. You are both waiting in the airport to check in for the return flight home. A stranger comes up to you and gets talking. After a while he asks you to do him a favour - to take a small package with you for someone in London. For your troubles he's willing to pay quite a lot of money. At first you think it may contain drugs - but you have no proof. It could be a harmless present. The money he's offering is very tempting. What do you do?

7. A friend is a friend

Paul, my best friend, is gay, and now he is not hiding it anymore. I can't hang around with him because all my other friends will think I'm that way as well.'
What would you do?

12. God's Tipp-Ex

It's highly likely that you have upset or hurt a friend at some time. It's equally likely that you've been upset by something a friend has done to you. When friends have an argument the immediate reaction is for them to ignore one another. If this continues the friends grow apart and the friendship dies.

After a bust up you might not want the other person to be your friend. The problem with holding a grudge is that it will destroy you! If you are not capable of forgiving a person – it's you who eventually suffer. Life is too short to hold grudges after the initial pain of the fight has faded.

There is another course of action open to you. You can arrange a meeting to talk the problem through, even apologise. Let go of past hurts and get rid of bad feeling. Although this is very difficult to do, be brave – phone or write, shake hands – even give a hug. Making up is not a sign of weakness but a sign of courage.

In what ways have you hurt people?

_____
_____
_____
_____
_____
_____
_____
_____

In what ways have people hurt you?

_____
_____
_____
_____
_____
_____
_____

Tipp-Ex-ing away

'_Forgive us our trespasses, as we forgive those who trespass against us_'
• where does this come from?
• what is meant by trespass?
• what does this imply when we ask for forgiveness?

In many ways you can hurt your friendship with God. Anything you do to God or your neighbour that shows a lack of love or respect is a sin. In life it is very easy to have arguments with people. Likewise it is very easy to sin. Sin can be likened to a puncture in a tyre. A puncture is a lack of rubber and allows air to pass through. Sin is a lack of love.

God is your ultimate friend and because He is all forgiving – whatever sins you have committed – He is able to forgive. He just Tipp-Ex's them away and they are forgiven and forgotten. However, there are some conditions to this:

1. you have to recognise your sins and ask for forgiveness

2. you must try not to commit the sins again

3. you have to forgive other people their mistakes against you.

These are difficult conditions and although you might not always be able to keep them – God asks you to try.

Jesus' hurts

There were many occasions when Jesus was hurt.
- Peter's denial at knowing Him – this was a breaking of trust and a promise
- the nine lepers who didn't give thanks for curing them – lack of thanks
- Judas – rejection and betrayal of Jesus
- the traders at the temple – lack of awe for a holy place
- the storm on the sea – despair and lack of trust in Jesus
- after feeding of the 5000 some wanted more – being used
- the bread of life – disbelief in the Eucharist
- healing of the paralytic – disbelief in Jesus' power to forgive and heal.

Jesus' forgiveness

There are many examples of Jesus' forgiveness of people.
- the parable of the prodigal son – the father waited for the son to return, he didn't force him to come home but when he did and asked for forgiveness the father forgave him completely
- the good thief who died with Jesus on the cross – the thief asked Jesus to remember him, and Jesus did by forgiving his sins
- Mary Magdalene – who led a sinful life, when she cried on realising the life she led and expressed her emotion, Jesus responded by forgiving her
- the adulteress – after admitting her wrong-doing, Jesus' forgiveness proves more embracing than that of others.

Jesus has all authority from His Father in heaven to forgive sins. Jesus passed authority to forgive sins to a few of His chosen followers when He said, 'Those whose sins you forgive, they are forgiven. Those whose sins you retain, they are retained'.

Who did He give this authority to, when and why?

_____
_____
_____
_____
_____
_____

This authority has been passed down through the priesthood in the Sacrament of Reconciliation (or Confession or Penance – as it is also called). Jesus work through the priest to forgive sins. One of the signs used in the sacrament is extending his hands as he forgives you in God's name.

In what ways could you symbolise the meaning of Confession or Reconciliation?

_____
_____
_____
_____
_____
_____
_____

Confession is dreaded by most people and this fear has prevented them from going. Confession is only a meeting or encounter with a waiting, forgiving Father who heals, forgives and strengthens for the future.

Sacrament of Reconciliation

People find many reasons for not going to Confession.

■ I don't know what to do
■ I don't know what to say
■ I know the priest and he'll tell people my sins
■ I know the priest and I won't be able to look him in the face again

This is a guide to help you through the first two excuses. It is only a suggested format but give it a go.

Steps in going to Confession

1. Prepare before you go in

Have a reasonable idea of what you are going to say. This is sometimes called an examination of conscience – deciding what sins you are going to confess (see What Causes Hurt and Division).

2. Going in

There are different sorts of Confessional (the box you go into!). Some have a screen between you and the priest and it means that he can't recognise you! The alternative is being face to face with the priest. Although this means that he will see you it is more natural and, believe it or not, allows a freer and easier Confession.

3. Bless me father

'Bless me father for I have sinned. This is ----------- (how long?) since my last Confession'. The traditional thing to say – or say 'hello' and just talk naturally.

4. Confess your sins

Just talk naturally and freely and the priest will help, if you want.

5. The priest will talk to you

Don't worry, he won't shout at you or be angry and he certainly won't be shocked as there probably isn't a sin he hasn't heard before. He will then give you penance – something to do to make up for your sins. This usually takes the form of prayers to say.

6. Say the Act of Contrition

If you don't know one already you can say:

'O my God, I am sorry for all my sins, for not loving others and not loving You. Help me to live like Jesus and not to sin again. Amen.'

7. Absolution

The priest will absolve (or forgive) you of your sins, and bless you.

8. Farewell

You say thank you and goodbye.

9. Do your penance

Outside you do whatever the priest has given in penance.

What causes hurt and division

■ judging someone
■ talking behind a person's back
■ cynicism and sarcasm
■ breaking trust or promises
■ not playing a proper and active part in a friendship or relationship – being passive
■ taking another for granted
■ spreading rumours or gossiping
■ lack of respect for another's principles, personality or body
■ lack of respect for what belongs to another – not returning things borrowed, stealing or vandalism
■ treating others in a way that you wouldn't want to be treated yourself (Lk 6:31)

---

13. Darkness & Light
A Reflection on Penance

Introduction: The reflection is based around light and darkness – symbols of good and sin, and exploring the areas of sin in our lives and making a commitment to live a life of light based on Jesus.

Assemble and **become quiet**

Penitential hymn

Scripture reading (Rom 7:15-24)

Six candidates, representing everyone else, take part in this service. Each holds a lighted candle in a dark room. Everyone else has an unlit candle.

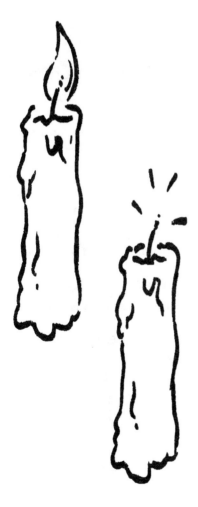

Candidate 1: There have been times in my life when I haven't been as good a son/daughter as I might have been. I have caused problems at home. I have been quarrelsome, lacking in understanding and sensitivity towards my parents. This has caused hurt. At these times I sinned, destroying the light of Christ.
(*Pause, then blow out the candle*).

Candidate 2: There have been times when I haven't made the most of opportunities given to me. I have wasted time. I haven't always used to the full the talents God has given to me, particularly in regard to school. I've been lazy. At these times I sinned, destroying the light of Christ.
(*Pause, then blow out the candle*).

Candidate 3: There have been times when I've been unfair in my relationships. I have broken promises and divulged confidences and secrets. I have talked about my friends to other friends in a damaging, belittling manner. I have ignored people. I have been choosy. I have been a bad example to my own peer group. At these times I sinned, destroying the light of Christ.
(*Pause, then blow out the candle*).

Candidate 4: There have been times when I compromised on my own beliefs and convictions in order to be popular; in language which has degraded the beauty and gift of sex; in running down my own religion to impress; in group activities like drinking, smoking, just to seek attention. At these times I sinned, destroying the light of Christ.
(*Pause, then blow out the candle*).

Candidate 5: There have been times when I fell down on my duties as a young Christian. I have seldom put others before myself. I've been careless in prayer. Pride and other interests have kept me away from Confession. Cynicism towards the clergy or lack of effort has kept me away from or led me to being bored at Mass. At these times I sinned, destroying the light of Christ.
(*Pause, then blow out the candle*).

Candidate 6: There have been times when I've been dishonest with the people around me. I've told lies for the sake of personal gain. I haven't always respected others or their belongings. I've been slow in returning things I've borrowed. On occasions I've tried to avoid paying my own way. At these times I sinned, destroying the light of Christ.
(*Pause, then blow out the candle*).

(*After a brief period of silence*)

Priest: Lord, it is dark. Your light has gone out, and so has its reflection on the people and the things around me. In darkness we lose our way. It frightens us. We walk hesitantly, not knowing what is around us. We feel alone and nervous, confused and very unsure of ourselves. We fumble frantically for a way out of a dark house, room or corridor, especially if the surroundings are not familiar. Lord, take away the darkness in our lives. You who, through your Resurrection, overcame all darkness, all sin and all evil. Let your light shine again in our lives. Show us the way.

(*Each candidate now promises to change the area of his/her life in which there has been sin, promising with the help of God's grace, faithfulness and courage in being better. Each relights the candle, symbolising Christ's presence in their life now.*)

Candidate 1: Lord, I promise to be a better person at home, making a special effort to love, honour and respect my parents, thereby bringing a little more of your light into our world.
(*Pause, then relight the candle.*)

Candidate 2: Lord, I promise, with your help, to respect life better, especially my own. I will use my talents more fully in the future for your service and for the services of my fellow man, thereby spreading a little more of your light in our world.
(*Pause, then relight the candle.*)

Candidate 3: Lord, I will be a better friend in the future. I will try to be natural when relating with others, avoiding attention-seeking and unnecessary loudness. I will be careful not to belittle people by talking about them to others. In this way I will spread a little more of your light in our world.
(*Pause, then relight the candle.*)

Candidate 4: Lord, I will try to stand up for what I believe in without being brash or hurtful. I will strive to become a true and real person. In this way I will spread a little more of your light in our world.
(*Pause, then relight the candle.*)

Candidate 5: Lord, in the future, with your help, I will try to be a better Christian. I will stay close to you in prayer and through the Sacraments, knowing that these will give me the strength and courage to be better. I will be charitable. In this way I will spread a little more of your light in our world.
(*Pause, then relight the candle.*)

Candidate 6: Lord, I will try to become aware of the need for justice in the world. I will be more honest. I will respect others and their belongings. I will avoid deceitfulness and trickery. In this way I will spread a little more of your light in our world.
(*Pause, then relight the candle.*)

Priest: Though we are sinners we have been saved in Christ. He is the light that never goes out. So long as we can focus on His light there is hope. He is waiting to take us back to Himself, to reconcile us with the Father. We can experience His touch of healing and forgiveness in the Sacrament of Reconciliation, through the power of the Holy Spirit.

(*A time of silence should then follow, perhaps with light music – then there can follow an examination of conscience.*)

Priest:

■ Am I happy with who I am or am I always wishing I were a different person in looks or lifestyle?

■ Is my life full of 'ifs' with regard to my family, talents, riches, intelligence and parents?

■ Do I waste time, useless daydreaming, do I avail of, and accept, the many opportunities given to me at school?

■ Do I live for the present or am I always looking forward to some great event in the future?

■ Am I selfish, always looking for more than I have, money, clothes, entertainment?

■ Do I easily get bored, maybe because something doesn't suit me? Is there a balance between leisure and work?

■ Do I respect people and their property, am I caring and honest?

■ Am I sincere, truthful and do I keep promises?

■ Am I aware of those less well off, the poor, handicapped, those who seem dull and ugly?

Music: 'Lay Your hands gently upon us.'

(*As it plays the priest lays hands as a symbol of God's forgiveness, and anoints with oil. Then everyone lights their own candles as a symbol of saying 'yes' and as a sign of being reconciled with and forgiven by the Father. Each person's light is a personal 'yes' to a new life in Christ. There should also be an opportunity for the priest to hear confessions.*)

14. Don't Forget Me!

Going to Mass

Going to Mass every Sunday is a central part of the life of a practising Catholic. The Mass has many important aspects; it's a:
- re-enactment of the Last Supper
- remembering and making present the sacrifice of Jesus at Calvary
- remembrance of Jesus
- way of getting close to Jesus in His Body and Blood
- celebration involving the community
- thanksgiving for everything God has given us

The celebration of Mass is at the very heart of the Catholic community. A word associated with the Mass is Communion, which means sharing. In Holy Communion, an important part of the Mass, there is sharing or communion not only with the life of Christ but with the other members of the faith community.

Meals

Nowadays it is very common for people to eat in front of the TV or on the street. There are so many take-aways and fast food places that people literally 'eat on their feet in the street'. People often eat like this because they are in a hurry.

Meals, however, are not only times when we fuel the body with nutrients. They are also social occasions when people share together. The family shares its meals together at certain times, such as Sunday lunch or Christmas dinner. At conferences and important meetings there is often a formal dinner when people dress up and share a meal together. A dinner dance is another example of people getting together socially. Also, it's really nice going out for a meal or being invited to someone's house for dinner. Wedding receptions, birthdays, and funerals are often associated with gatherings of people and food.

Jesus chose a meal with His disciples to share not only bread and wine but something much more precious and special. Through the bread and wine He offers us His Body and Blood to keep us alive spiritually.

The Last Supper

Just before the Passover, Jesus and His disciples were gathered together in the upper room for the Passover meal.

Jesus took some bread, and when He had said the blessing He broke it and gave it to His disciples. 'Take it and eat;' He said 'this is my Body.' Then He took a cup of wine and said, 'Drink all of you from this, for this is my Blood, the Blood of the New Covenant, which is to be poured out for many for the forgiveness of sins. From now on, I tell you, I shall not drink wine until the day I drink the new wine with you in the Kingdom of my Father.'

The Last Supper is re-enacted in the Mass as a reminder of Jesus giving His life for us. Being at Mass and taking Communion allows us to come very close to Jesus.

Ordinary food is broken up and taken into the cells of the body and eventually becomes part of us. When we receive the Eucharist we become part of the Body of Christ.

The Mass is made up of two main parts: the Liturgy of the Word and the Liturgy of the Eucharist.

During the **Liturgy of the Word** we as a congregation say prayers and read passages from the Bible. There's a first reading from the Old Testament, a second reading from the New Testament and a Gospel reading. The Liturgy of the Word basically involves God speaking to us in the Bible readings and through the sermon or homily, which is a 'breaking of the Word', and we as a congregation then respond to God in prayers.

After the Creed, which states our beliefs, we offer prayers as a community in response to the invitations made in the bidding prayers.

During the **Liturgy of the Eucharist**, we make an offering to God and we celebrate God offering Himself to us. During this part the Word is made 'flesh' for us to eat.

Many symbols are used during Mass, so watch out for them:

■ offering the bread ('This is for you, take this') represents Jesus sharing His life with you
■ washing of hands to symbolise cleanliness
■ mingling of water and wine, represents how you are absorbed within Jesus and shows His oneness with you
■ breaking the bread – Jesus 'broken' on the Cross
■ sign of peace – shows fellowship with the rest of the community
■ the word Mass is Latin for 'dismissal'– you are being asked to go forth in Christ to the community to do His work

What symbols could you use to represent the meaning of the Eucharist?

With so many good things going for the Mass, it's surprising that many people do not like going. What are the reasons for this? Some turn-offs may include:

■ it's too boring
■ it's too long
■ there's too much singing
■ I prefer to be in bed or watching TV
■ I don't understand what's going on
■ I don't know what the priest is on about in the sermon

Do you agree with some or all of these points?

Mass is boring!

What things would you change in the Mass to make it more meaningful to you?

_____
_____
_____
_____

What do you like about the Mass?

_____
_____
_____

Why do you think it's important to go to Mass every Sunday?

_____
_____
_____
_____

15. Bread & Wine
A Reflection on the Eucharist

This reflection gives the Eucharist its historical Old Testament setting, drawing out the idea of sacrifice, Passover, remembrance and salvation.

Leader: Jesus was a Jew, who each year joined with the people in celebrating the Passover Feast. This is an important feast because it calls to mind the passing over of the Jewish people from Egypt to Israel – from slavery to freedom.

First Reader: *This reading is taken from the Book of Exodus 12:21-28.*

Moses summoned all the elders of Israel and said to them, 'Go and choose animals from the flock on behalf of your families, and kill the Passover victim. Then take a spray of hyssop, dip it in the blood that is in the basin, and with the blood from the basin touch the lintel and the two doorposts. Let none of you venture out of the house till morning. Then, when Yahweh goes through Egypt to strike it, and sees the blood on the lintel and on the two doorposts, He will pass over the door and not allow the destroyer to enter your homes and strike. You must keep these rules as an ordinance for all time for you and your children. When you enter the land that Yahweh is giving you, as He promised, you must keep to this ritual. And when your children ask you, 'What does this ritual mean?' you will tell them, 'It is the sacrifice of the Passover in honour of Yahweh who passed over the houses of the sons of Israel in Egypt, and struck Egypt but spared our houses.' And the people bowed down and worshipped. The sons of Israel then departed, and they obeyed. They carried out the orders Yahweh had given to Moses and Aaron.

Leader: So the Israelites were saved through the blood of the lamb. They were asked to remember this great act of God every year – they and their children. Through celebrating the Passover Feast, Salvation would continue to be theirs and through the celebration Salvation was to be passed on from generation to generation. In other words, as often as the Passover was celebrated the work of their redemption was carried on. Every celebration carried the reality of the first celebration held in Egypt.

Reader 2: *This reading is taken from the Book of Deuteronomy 16:1-3.*

Observe the month of Ahib and celebrate the Passover for Yahweh your God, because it was in the month of Abib that Yahweh your God brought you out of Egypt by night. You must sacrifice a Passover from your flock or herd for Yahweh your God in the place where Yahweh chooses to give His name a home... So, you will remember, all the days of your life, the day you came out of the land of Egypt.

Hymn: 'Jesus, the Faithful One.'

Leader: Jesus chose this feast of Passover to give us the Eucharist. The great gift of Himself for all humankind for all generations.

Reader 3: *This reading is taken from Luke 22:9; 14-16; 19-20.*
(This may also be mimed simultaneously by 12 people using bread and a chalice)

Jesus sent Peter and John, saying, 'Go and make the preparations for us to eat the Passover'... When the hour came He took His place at table, and the apostles with Him. And He said to them, 'I have longed to eat this Passover with you before I suffer, because I tell you, I shall not eat it again until it is fulfilled in the Kingdom of God'... Then He took some bread, and when He had given thanks, broke it and gave it to them, saying, 'This is my body which will be given for you; do this as a memorial of me.' He did the same with the cup after supper, and said, 'This is the cup of my blood, the blood of the new and everlasting covenant. It will be shed for you and for all so that sins may be forgiven. Do this in memory of me.'

Leader: Jesus Himself became the New Passover lamb. The lamb's blood would be sprinkled on the Cross next day at Calvary. As the Jews were saved from slavery and oppression in Egypt, now all Christians baptised in Christ's death and resurrection would be saved from sin and eternal death.

Jesus said, 'Do this in memory of me'. So as the Jews in their yearly Passover Feast made the saving act of God present and real, the Mass, each time it is celebrated, makes the reality of Calvary, the saving act of Christ, present to all who want it. As often as the Mass is celebrated the work of our redemption is carried on through the elements of bread and wine, the bread representing the lamb of God and the wine His blood. 'This is the lamb of God who takes away the sins of the world. Happy are those who are called to His supper.'

Reader 4: *This reading is taken from the First Letter of St Paul to the Corinthians 10:16-17; 11:23-26.*

The blessing cup that we bless is a communion with the blood of Christ, and the bread that we break is a communion with the body of Christ. The fact that there is only one loaf means that, though there are many of us, we form a single body because we all have a share in this one loaf... For this is what I received from the Lord, and in turn passed on to you: that on the same night that he was betrayed, the Lord Jesus took some bread, and thanked God for it and broke it, and he said, 'This is my body, which is for you, do this as a memorial of me.' In the same way He took the cup after supper, and said, 'This cup is the new covenant in my blood. Whenever you drink it, do this as a memorial of me.'

Hymn: 'When we eat this bread'

Activity: Finish the reflection by sharing together:
- a meal
- stories told by parents, grandparents or elderly neighbours (asremembrance)
- photographs of themselves when very young

16. A Never-Ending Story

A brief history of time

In history lessons at school, you can look back at how people lived thousands of years ago in ancient civilisations. History can give us a sense of identity and purpose by allowing us to see what people did in the past and how it affects what we do today. To understand why we do things in a particular way we need to look back and see why it was done originally, how it has changed, and the reasons why it changed.

To understand the meaning of Confirmation you need to know about its history.

History of our faith

Our faith has a history, and our history book is the Bible. The Bible contains the history of God working in our world and how He communicated His message to His people.

Write down the names of anyone you can recall mentioned in the Bible?

What stories are associated with them?

As far as Confirmation is concerned its origins can be traced back to Pentecost when the Apostles received the Holy Spirit in a special way. The Holy Spirit helped and guided the Apostles to spread the message of God.

What can you remember of the story of Pentecost?

Early Christian communities

People who heard and believed the message of Jesus formed the first members of the Christian Church. Inspired by His life and teachings they tried to follow Jesus' message by living good and faithful lives. Christians were in the minority, being surrounded by many non-believers. Like most minorities, they produced a close knit community. Unlike many other close communities, the early Christians cared for anyone who needed help, be they Christian or not.

They were such shining examples of Jesus' message that many non-Christians were inspired by them and wanted to join the community. However, people were allowed to join only after they understood the implications of being a Christian. To help them understand, there was a period of preparation when the interested people, or candidates, were instructed in the faith by a member of the community. When the candidate was prepared and ready they were initiated into the community.

A person who joins a group may undergo a process of initiation. If you start work in a new company the initiation may involve being shown around and introduced to the staff to familiarise you with the organisation. If you join a street gang you may undergo an initiation such as taking an oath to stand by the other members. Likewise, to join the Church you need to go through an initiation ceremony.

Through the centuries the initiation ceremony of the Church has changed. At first only adults were allowed to join fully as they were able to understand the responsibilities being taken on.

In the early Church, the initiation (or Baptism) started with the Bishop blessing the baptismal waters. The candidates publicly renounced Satan, then they were anointed with the oil of Catechumens by a priest. The Baptism then took place and involved the person being totally immersed in the water. The newly baptised person then put on a white garment which was a sign of a new start in their lives – a re-birth.

Often there was a second anointing which was performed by the Bishop. He laid hands on the newly baptised people and prayed that they may be filled with the Holy Spirit, then he poured consecrated oil on their heads and embraced them as a sign of peace.

The person was admitted into full communion with the Church by celebrating the breaking of bread or Eucharist. The ceremony therefore involved not only Baptism but Confirmation and the Eucharist.

Safe to come out

The Christian Church has been persecuted throughout its history at various times and in various places. This was especially so when it first started.

Why should something that promotes peace be persecuted?

In the fourth century the Church was no longer outlawed, and this resulted in many more people coming forward to become Christians. With an increase in the faithful community, Bishops could not preside over all Baptisms, so priests conducted the Baptisms. The final anointing was then reserved for the Bishops to perform at a later date. This later anointing became a confirming of the candidate's Baptism.

The Church continued to grow and with the increase in the number of people becoming Christians the time between Baptism and anointing increased as the Bishop now had so many people to visit. Gradually the two ceremonies were regarded as separate actions. By the ninth century the word Confirmation was used to describe just the action of the Bishop and became a separate Sacrament.

Infant Baptism

Most Baptisms in the Catholic Church involve infants or babies and if you hear of an adult being baptised you might think it rather strange. Even in the early Church infant baptisms were common. With the increase in the number of people becoming Christians there was an increase in the number of Christian marriages and births. Hygiene and inadequate medical care meant that infant mortality was high. Quite often children died in infancy or childhood.

Parents became worried that their children might die before they were able to enter the Church. They wanted their babies baptised in case anything happened to them. The long preparation for Baptism was therefore no longer required.

Gradually the three Sacraments of Baptism, Confirmation and Eucharist became separated. Baptism became a Sacrament which marked the initial entry into the Church of the infant. The parents and godparents would take the baptismal vows on behalf of the infant and would promise to bring up the child in the Christian faith. Eucharist became First Holy Communion, and Confirmation became a Sacrament which marked that the person could understand the implications of becoming a Christian and confirmed their faith by taking their baptismal vows for themselves.

Journey in faith

During your life you've undergone many changes – from a baby to a toddler, a toddler to a child and finally into a young adult. During these periods your interests and knowledge has undergone quite a lot of change.

If you allow it, your faith can undergo development as well. When you were very young your parents looked after your religious life, but eventually you have to take the responsibility. Your life can be looked upon as a journey, and your religious life can be looked upon as a journey in faith.

The Bible tells the stories of many people's faith journey. Part of your journey in faith has involved this Confirmation programme. How prepared are you to take the responsibility of your journey in faith? This story may help you.

Always keep your goal in sight and you'll never get lost.

A group of children decided to go for a walk in the countryside. They started from on top of a hill and looked out over the surroundings. They spotted another hill about ten miles away. They didn't have a map and decided to walk to the hill in a straight line. They started off and soon found that it wasn't possible to get there directly because they met various obstructions such as fences and streams. All the time they were walking they kept their destination in sight.

Along one of the roads, a car pulled up and the driver wound down the window. The driver stuck out his head and said that he was lost and asked where they were. One of the children said that they didn't know. The driver said that they must be as lost as he was. The same child said, 'We are not lost, we know where we come from and know where we are going. How can we be lost?'

Your faith journey checklist ✓

What are your goals in life?

- money, riches, fame
- happiness, peace
-
-

How are you going to prepare to achieve your goals?
- wait for good fortune
- work gradually towards success
-
-

If you were going exploring – What do you need to take with you?
- a map
- food and nourishment
- companions
- money
-
-

What would you need to take on your journey in faith?
-
-
-
-
-
-

If you needed help on your faith journey who could you ask?
-
-
-
-
-

17. Powerful Signs

During your Confirmation you will experience some very powerful symbolism. For you to understand and benefit from what is happening it's worth finding out what they all mean.

Laying on of hands

One of the first symbols is the **laying on of hands**. This is a very ancient custom which continues to feature in our daily lives.

Can you think of times when the laying on of hands is used today and the meaning behind the action?

Laying on of hands in Scripture

Jesus and the children. People brought little children to Him to lay His hands on and say a little prayer. The disciples turned them away, but Jesus said, 'Let the little children alone, and do not stop them from coming to me; for it is to such as these that the kingdom of heaven belongs.' Then He laid His hands on them and went on His way. *(Mt 19:13-15)*

Barnabas and Saul are selected for a mission. One day while they were offering worship to the Lord and keeping fast, the Holy Spirit said, 'I want Barnabas and Saul set apart for the work to which I have called them.' So it was that after fasting and prayer they laid their hands on them and sent them off. *(Acts 13:2-3)*

A sense of sharing. When the apostles in Jerusalem heard that Samaria had accepted the word of God, they sent Peter and John to them and they went down there, and prayed for the Samaritans to receive the Holy Spirit, for as yet he had not come down on any of them: they had only been baptised in the name of the Lord Jesus. Then they laid hands on them, and they received the Holy Spirit. *(Acts 8:14-16)*

Anointing

Oil has great value in our society and it is keenly searched for within the earth and under the sea. Oil is used for heating, providing power, giving light, healing, embrocation (that is rubbing oil into the skin). When oil is rubbed into the body it provides warmth, and allows better circulation to the skin and muscles.

Anointing in the Church

In **Baptism** a child or adult is anointed with the oil of Catechumens to symbolise having 'strength in the power of Christ' and with oil of Chrism, to be anointed 'Priest, Prophet and King' a sign of being specially chosen and set apart for special work.

In **Anointing of the Sick**, the priest anoints the body and says, 'May the Lord in His love and mercy help you with the grace of the Holy Spirit.'

In **Confirmation** the candidate is anointed with the oil of Chrism and sealed with the gifts of the Holy Spirit.

In **Holy Orders**, the Bishop or priest is anointed with oil.

On all these occasions, the idea of strength, understanding, service to life in the Church, to take on the mission of Christ in the world, is celebrated.

Anointing in the Scriptures

Anointing contains the sense of being set aside for a mission, as these readings from Scripture show.

David is selected and anointed as King. 'God said to Samuel, "Fill your horn with oil and go. I am sending you to Jesse of Bethlehem, for I have chosen myself a king among his sons." Samuel did as God had asked. When he arrived, Jesse showed him seven of his sons, but God told Samuel that none of these had been chosen by Him to be King. Samuel then asked Jesse, "Are these all the sons you have?" Jesse said, "There is still one left, the youngest; he is out looking after the sheep." Then Samuel said to Jesse, "Send for him; we will not sit down to eat until he comes."
Jesse had him sent for, a boy of fresh complexion, with fine eyes and pleasant bearing. God said, "Come, anoint him, for this is one." At this Samuel took the horn of oil and anointed him where he stood with his brothers; and the spirit of God seized on David and stayed with him from that day on.' (1 Sam 16:1-13)

At the **Synagogue at Nazareth**. 'The Spirit of the Lord has been given to me for He has anointed me. He sent me to bring good news to the poor, to proclaim liberty to captives and to the blind new sight. To set the down trodden free, to proclaim the Lord's year of favour.' (Lk 4:16)

In these passages, there is an idea of a job to be done and a mission to be accomplished.

The oil of Chrism is made of olive oil and sweet smelling balsam. It is consecrated, with the oil of Catechumens and oil of the Sick, each year by the Bishop on Holy Thursday morning. The oil of Chrism has an attractive smell which reminds us that the life of a Christian is to be good and attractive. The consecration on Holy Thursday is to remind us that we are confirmed into the death and resurrection of Christ.

Sign of peace

In Confirmation the sign of peace given by the Bishop to the candidates has special significance. The Bishop is the sign of unity of the whole Diocese and represents the wider Church, reminding us that we are not just a local group but belong to a worldwide community. The sign of peace symbolises that we belong to a wider community and that we should be on good terms with others.

In the community we are called to live in peace, gentleness and consideration with all others in the community.

18. Confirmation Away-Day
The Gifts of the Holy Spirit

Lord, we thank you for bringing us together on this special occasion. During this day together, help us to share our faith with one another and to come to a deeper understanding of the meaning and role of the Holy Spirit in our lives. Amen.

Find the Holy Spirit

Write down what you understand by the meaning of the word 'spirit'?

Find the Holy Spirit in the Old Testament

For each of the readings write down the role that the Holy Spirit is playing

---

■ **Reading 1: Creation of the world** *Gen 1:1-2*

'In the beginning God created the heavens and the earth. Now the earth was a formless void, there was darkness over the deep, and the spirit of God hovered over the water.'

What was the Holy Spirit doing at the beginning of time?

■ **Reading 2: Creation of man** *Gen 2:7*

'God fashioned man of dust from the soil. Then he breathed into his nostrils a breath of life, and thus man became a living being.'

In what way did the Spirit change the dust?

■ **Reading 3: The day of the Lord** *Joel 2:28*

'After this I will pour out my Spirit on all mankind; your sons and daughters shall prophesy, and your old men shall dream dreams and your young men shall see visions.'

How does the Holy Spirit change people?

Find the Holy Spirit in the New Testament

■ Reading 4: The annunciation *Lk 1: 26-35*

The angel Gabriel was sent to Mary to announce the coming of the Lord to her as a baby. 'And the angel said to her, "The Holy Spirit will come upon you, and the power of the Most High will overshadow you; therefore the child to be born will be called holy, the Son of God".'

The Holy Spirit can change people. In what ways did He change Mary?

■ Reading 7: Jesus in the synagogue in Nazareth *Lk 4:18-19*

'Returning to Nazareth, His home town, Jesus read the scroll of Isaiah: "The Spirit of the Lord is upon me, because He has chosen me to bring good news to the poor. He has send me to proclaim liberty to the captives and recovery of sight to the blind, to set free the oppressed and announce that the time has come when the Lord will save His people". Then He said, "Today this scripture has been fulfilled in your hearing".'

What did Jesus mean by this and what role did the Holy Spirit play?

■ Reading 5: Jesus' Baptism *Mk 1:10-11*

'As Jesus came out of the water of the Jordan, the Holy Spirit descended upon Him in bodily form like a dove; and a voice came from heaven "Thou art my beloved Son, with thee I am well pleased".'

This event marked a turning point in Jesus' life. In what ways did His life change?

■ Reading 8: Last Supper *Jn 14:16-17*

At the Last Supper, the night before He died, Jesus told His followers not to be afraid. He was leaving them, but His Father would send them a counsellor to be with them forever.

Who was this counsellor and what difference would he make to the followers?

■ Reading 10: Jesus' mission in the world *Matt 28:18-20*

After the resurrection, just before He ascended into heaven, Jesus commissioned His Apostles to carry His message to all nations. He told them to baptise all nations 'in the name of the father, and of the Son and of the Holy Spirit'.

How is the Holy Spirit to be passed on to others?

■ Reading 6: Jesus in the desert *Matt 4:1-11*

'The Holy Spirit led Jesus into the desert, where He spent forty days in prayer and fasting. The devil came to him and said "If you are the Son of God, command these stones to become loaves of bread". Even though Jesus was hungry he wouldn't be tempted. The devil then tried to test Him by asking Jesus to prove Himself and offering Him riches if He worshipped Satan. Jesus resisted the temptations and said, "You shall worship the Lord your God and Him only shall you serve".'

In what ways did the Spirit help Jesus resist the temptations?

■ Reading 9: Jesus' last breath on the Cross *Jn 19:30*

When Jesus had received the vinegar, He said, 'It is finished; and He bowed his head and gave up the Spirit'.

What was the importance of the Spirit in Jesus' life?

■ Reading 11: Pentecost *Acts 2:1-4*

Read this passage from the Bible about the coming of the Holy Spirit to the Apostles.

In what ways did the Holy Spirit change the Apostles?

If you watch the news you may wonder what is happening to the earth. There are riots, killings, thefts, muggings, kidnappings, pollution and destruction. You may wonder where the Holy Spirit is working to produce good effects. The news often highlights bad happenings but there are plenty of examples of people doing good. The Holy Spirit is still working in God's people today.Read the examples below and see if you can answer these questions.

Mother Teresa

• what do you know about Mother Teresa?

• what sort of work did she do?

• where did she carry out her work?

• did she have any helpers?

• what made her do such difficult work?

• what part did the Holy Spirit play in her life?

Central America

• what do you know about the people of central America?

• are most of them rich or poor?

• how is the Church trying to help the people?

• have you heard of Archbishop Romero and El Salvador? What do these names mean to you?

• how has the Holy Spirit helped all the people suffering there at the moment and why do people risk their life for justice?

Bob Geldof and Band-Aid

• find out about Bob Geldof and Band-Aid?

• what did he try to do and how?

• did it make any difference to the starving?

• what part did the Holy Spirit play?

• can one person affect millions of others?

Lourdes

• what do you know about Lourdes and St Bernadette?

• in what ways is St Bernadette's life inspiring to people today?

• why do ill people go to Lourdes today?

• why do healthy people go to Lourdes?

South Africa

• what do you know about the politics of South Africa?

• who have been the people who have tried to change the situation there and bring justice?

• what role has the Holy Spirit played in that country and around the world to bring justice?

Communist countries

• what recent changes have there been in the Soviet Union and the other communist countries?

• how was the Church treated before the recent changes?

• what kept the people faithful even though they were persecuted?

What do you understand by
the word 'gift'?

_____

When are gifts or presents
given?

_____

What's it like when you receive
a gift you like?

_____

What's it like when you give a
present?

_____

What's meant by a gifted
person?

_____

What sort of gifts or talents
have you got?

_____

Which talents do you
use?

_____

Which talents or gifts would you
like to have?

_____

Gifts of the Holy Spirit

The Holy Spirit gives us seven gifts, in a special way, at Confirmation. The gifts are given to help us grow in love and act as God wants us to act. The gifts are to be used and shared with other people.

The gifts are:

Understanding
• the gift of knowing the meaning of God's will for us.

Wisdom
• the ability to think and act using our knowledge, experience, understanding and insight.

Right judgment
• this gift helps us to know what to do, especially when we are faced with difficult situations.

Knowledge
• awareness gained by experience and learning.

Courage
• this gives us the strength to do what is right no matter how hard it may be.

Reverence
• this gift gives us the power to love God and our neighbour as we should.

Wonder and awe
• this gift gives us the power to remember the greatness of God and helps us to have a horror of offending God who has loved us so much.

The gifts of the Holy Spirit can affect, in a positive way, whatever you do. They are not, however, magical powers; they are strengths that help you grow in your Christian life. The gifts are there for you to use – they don't work automatically, you have to call upon them. In each of the stories given below answer the questions and explain how you would apply a particular gift.

Wisdom

Imagine you are the wealthy parent of a young child. Your child comes to you asking constantly for things such as new clothes, money to go out, records etc. You can afford to buy your child anything he or she desires.

■ do you give him/her everything that is asked for?

■ if not, why?

■ how would you decide on what to give and what not to give?

■ how would you apply **wisdom** to this situation?

Understanding

You have a friend who has an emotional problem. You think that she is blowing it out of all proportion but she keeps phoning you up and calling around telling you that same story everytime. You try to help by giving advice, but although she listens she never takes any advice. You can't see any way of helping her.

■ have you ever come across a similar situation?

■ if so, how did you deal with it?

■ should you carry on listening to her problems and trying to help even though you think it will never help?

■ how would you apply **understanding** to this situation?

Right judgment

A magistrate that you know sits in a court and dispenses justice. When he sits in the traffic court defendants appear before him who have committed traffic offences. One day he is judging a person caught for doing a U-turn in a particular street. The magistrate himself often does a U-turn at the same place as it saves time driving around the block.

■ can the magistrate still dispense justice when he has committed the same offence but has never been caught?

■ if so, why? Is this not hypocritical?

■ how can you apply **right judgment** in this situation?

Courage

You have a friend who is a black belt karate expert. At a party you're both at, trouble breaks out and things are looking as though they may get nasty. You want to leave but your friend decides to go in and sort things out.

You have another friend whose smaller sister is desperately ill in hospital. The doctors suspect bone cancer and she has to undergo a lot of painful treatment. However she is always happy and tries to cheer up her parents and other children in the ward.

■ which of the two people, the karate expert or the little girl is showing more courage?

■ explain your answer.

■ does courage always mean showing physical strength?

■ in what ways can you apply **courage** in your life?

Knowledge

A neighbour's son of about your age is a bit of a swot. Whenever you call around to suggest going out he says that he wants to study. He appears more interested in reading about nature than going out for a walk in the country. He gets all his information from books and watching TV documentaries rather than experiencing it for himself.

■ is it good enough for someone to have lots of knowledge from books rather than from experience?

■ if not, why?

■ is it good enough to have knowledge of Jesus' message without going out and putting it into practice? Explain your answer.

■ how should we apply **knowledge**?

Reverence

A class mate of your is always bragging about things she has done and people she's met, and parties that she's been to, and countries that she's visited. It wouldn't be so bad if the stories were interesting but she tells them again and again. It's really getting on your nerves as she always seems to pick on you to talk to.

■ how do you deal with someone like this. You don't really want to be rude but it's driving you mad.

■ how can you apply the gift of **reverence** to this person?

Wonder and awe

You are a fan of a particular mega pop star. On the day you're due to see him in concert you pop into a quiet coffee bar. There's hardly anyone in there – but you are amazed to see this pop singer on his own having a coffee – apparently getting away from it all. You often dreamt of meeting him – but you are dumb-struck.

■ do you go over to talk to him? Explain your answer.

■ how do you feel seeing him?

■ who are the people that you would be in **wonder** and **awe** at if you saw or met them?

Celebration of Mass

Will the gifts of the Holy Spirit in Confirmation make a difference in my life?

Theme: The fruits of the Holy Spirit

In a sense the answer to this question was given many years ago by someone who did a lot of travelling in the early days of the Church – St Paul. As he moved from place to place he began to notice certain qualities or characteristics in the lives of individuals, families, communities who opened themselves up to the influence and power of the Holy Spirit. He named these 'fruits' of the Holy Spirit as being: love, joy, peace, patience, kindness, goodness, faithfulness, gentleness and self-control.

The seeds of these fruits are given in Confirmation but as with all seeds they need cultivation and care. Given care and human effort these fruits are guaranteed.

19. Play
The First Confirmation

Players: Narrator, Jesus, Mary, Peter, John, Mary Magdalene, Martha, James, Andrew, Philip, Thomas, Bartholomew, Matthew, James, Person 1, Person 2.

Narrator: Three days after Jesus was crucified, Mary Magdalene went to mourn outside the tomb of Jesus. She was surprised to see that the stone had been moved and that the body of Jesus had gone. However, Jesus, in the guise of a gardener, sees Mary and approaches her. At first she didn't recognise Him.

Jesus: Woman, why are you weeping?

Mary M: They have taken my Lord away and I don't know where they have put Him. Do you know where He is?

Jesus: Mary.

Mary M: (*now recognising Jesus*) Master. (*she goes to touch Him*)

Jesus: Do not cling to me, because I have not yet ascended to the Father. But go and find my disciples and tell them that I am ascending to my Father.

Narrator: Mary ran to the room where the disciples were hiding for fear of the Jews. Mary burst into the room full of excitement.

Mary: I have seen the Lord. He is risen.

Bartholomew: What are you talking about?

Mary M: Jesus is alive.

Narrator: Although the doors were closed, for fear of the Jews, everyone in the room became aware of a presence. Jesus suddenly appeared and stood in the midst of them. The disciples were at once astonished and pleased to see Him. Jesus then spoke.

Jesus: Peace be with you.

Narrator:	And Jesus showed them His hands and His side. The disciples were filled with joy, and Jesus said again,
Jesus:	Peace be with you.
Narrator:	Thomas, also known as the doubter, always wanted proof before he believed anything. He was absent when Jesus first appeared, when Thomas returned he was told the good news of the resurrection of Jesus.
Bartholomew:	Thomas, Jesus has risen from the dead. He was here and He spoke to us.
Thomas:	How do we know for certain that it was Jesus ? Unless I see the holes that the nails made in his hands and can put my finger into them, and unless I can put my hand into His side I refuse to believe.
Narrator:	Eight days later the disciples were in the house again and Thomas was with them. The doors were closed, but Jesus came in and stood among them.
Jesus:	Peace be with you. Thomas put your finger here; look, here are my hands. Give me your hand; put it into my side. Doubt no longer but believe.
Thomas:	My Lord and my God. I believe that it is you.
Jesus:	Thomas, you believe because you can see me. Happy are those who have not seen yet believe.
Narrator:	Jesus appeared to His followers on numerous occasions over the next forty days and spoke to them about the Kingdom of God. On one occasion they were sharing a meal together and He told them to expect the coming of the Holy Spirit.
Jesus:	Do not leave Jerusalem. Wait here for my Father will send you the Holy Spirit that I promised you. John baptised with water but you, not many days from now, will be baptised with the Holy Spirit. For soon I must leave.
John:	But why must you leave us?
Jesus:	I must return to my Father, but my Spirit will always be with you and you will be my witnesses not only in Jerusalem but throughout the whole world.

Narrator: Soon afterwards Jesus was lifted up into heaven and a cloud took Him from their sight. All Jesus' followers were gathered in Jerusalem praying and preparing to be confirmed in the Holy Spirit. Among them was Mary, the mother of Jesus, who was leading them in prayer.

Mary, Our Lady: Jesus, help us to continue your mission on earth. It is a difficult task and we welcome the coming of the Holy Spirit to help us in our work.

James: Lord, I do not know fully what you want of me. Give me the wisdom to know what you would like me to do.

Andrew: Jesus, I have problems in knowing how to carry out your will. Give me the understanding of how to carry out your wishes.

Philip: Lord, I am going to be put in difficult situations. Give me the gift of right judgment that I will know how to react when I have problems.

Matthew: Lord, I know I am a man and supposed to be brave, but I do feel frightened when carrying out your work. Give me the courage to speak out and spread your word.

James: Lord, sometimes I find it difficult to love my neighbour. Give me the gift to love my neighbour as I should love you.

Martha: Lord, sometimes I feel there is so much other work to do that I have little time for you. Give me the gift of wonder and awe that I might remember your greatness.

Narrator: Suddenly they heard what sounded like a powerful gust of wind from heaven, the noise of which filled the entire room in which they were sitting; and something appeared to them that seemed like tongues of fire; these separated and came to rest on the head of each of them. They were all filled with the Holy Spirit, and began to speak foreign languages as the Spirit gave them the gifts.
Before receiving the Holy Spirit, they were fearful and hiding in a room. After they received the Spirit, they burst out into the streets, proclaiming the word of God in many languages and everyone was amazed.

Person 1 in crowd: Surely, all these people speaking are Galileans. How are they able to speak all these foreign languages?

Person 2 in crowd: I think they have been drinking too much wine.

Narrator: Then Peter stood up and addressed the crowd in a loud voice.

Peter: People of Jerusalem, we are not drunk. On the contrary, this is what Joel the prophet, said: 'In the days to come I will pour out my Spirit on all mankind'. Jesus, the man, who you killed, is alive, raised by God and we are all witnesses to this. He promised to send the Holy Spirit to us and what you see before you is the outpouring of that Spirit.

Narrator: Hearing this the crowd was cut to the heart.

Person 2:   What must I do to receive the Holy Spirit too?

Peter: You must repent, believe in Jesus, and be baptised. Then you will be ready to be confirmed in the Holy Spirit.

Not the End
– but just the Beginning.

20. Just Do It

For better or worse

The world contains millions upon millions of young people. Some of them are far better off than you. They probably have a larger house, go on two or three holidays a year and get a lot more pocket-money to spend than you. The majority of the world's young people are however worse off than you. In many cases much worse off, and not only in terms of money.

The challenge

God challenges us to help the less fortunate than ourselves. Here are some examples of the less fortunate. What can you do to help your fellow young people?

Child labour

It has been estimated that there are more than 100 million child slaves in the world today. They can be found in India, Thailand, the Sudan, Philippines and many other countries. These children are exploited for labour. In Thailand there is an open market for children. 'Fisherwomen' tour the villages giving parents an advance on the wages of their children of about £12. The children are taken to Bangkok, where they are sold into sweatshops. The slave-traders charge around £135 for a 12 year old girl. The youngest may be seven years old. Most of Thailand's 7 million child workers do manual work, making carpets or wrapping sweets. The prettiest children work in the brothels. In the Sudan, boys go to work in the fields and girls into domestic slavery. A child sells for about £10.

In Europe, 200,000 Portuguese children, under 14 years old, work in bars, building sites and factories. In Naples, poor Italian girls make expensive shoes in airless basements with fumes of the adhesives they use. Child labour makes sense to some people; children come cheap, they can do various tasks, they don't form trade unions, they can be beaten and pushed around, and they are a renewable resource.

What can you do to help?

The starving millions

We all see the horrific pictures on the television news of African children who are starving to death literally in front of our eyes. Their bodies are like skeletons with pot bellies, and they haven't the strength to brush the flies away from them.

While the children of some countries haven't seen food for weeks or months, we in the so called 'developed' countries are preoccupied with the effects of eating too much. So many diets are available for people who just can't stop eating.

How many times have you said, 'I'm starving' when you haven't eaten for a couple of hours? Imagine not eating anything for a day, a week, or a month.

What can you do to help?

Drug addicts

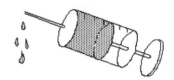

Despite posters and campaigns there continues to be a major problem with drug addicts. Most addicts are young people. You rarely find older addicts because they die early in life. If drug addicts don't overdose, they can die through infection caught through sharing dirty syringe needles. AIDS is rife among addicts.

The life of an addict is as low as you can get. To obtain money, addicts are known to steal money or break into Chemists to steal drugs. Many 'shoot up' in public lavatories, where many are found dead.

What can you do to help?

The homeless

Recently, the shop owners in the Strand, a fashionable street in London, got together to discuss what do about the homeless cluttering up their doorways and begging money of their customers. They met in the Savoy Hotel and discussed buying a French cleansing vehicle that showered the doorways with a water spray. They thought that when the 'tramps' were drenched they would feel so uncomfortable that they would move on 'to trouble' someone else!

When a representative from an organisation dealing with the homeless was interviewed he made the point that the majority of the so-called tramps were under 18 years old and were technically children. Would the shop traders do this to their own children?

Many children and young adults run away from home for many reasons. In some cases they come from large families and feel neglected, in some cases they have been abused. They go to large cities looking for work and instead fall prey to thugs, gangsters and pimps.

What can be done for them?

Ceaucescu's children

In Romania, a country in Eastern Europe, there were over 100,000 abandoned children in orphanages. They were locked up and forgotten about until the dictator Nicolae Ceausescu was overthrown by a popular revolution.

The children were malnourished and neglected, and were cramped into run-down, understaffed homes and institutions, short of food, medical supplies and above all of love, care and any form of stimulation.

At three years old many of the children were wrongly identified as 'irrecuperables' – the term Romanians use for children they believe to be beyond help. Some may not be handicapped at all, suffering only from deprivation; others will be backward, only mildly developmen-tally disabled; others will be both physically and mentally severely handicapped and in need of special care and attention which would give them a chance to develop and achieve a reasonable quality of life. But the homes for the 'irrecuperables' offer nothing but misery.

The country now faces so many social and economic problems that the abandoned children and the conditions in the orphanages are not necessarily a priority.

What can you do to help?

People who care

If your answer to the challenges is 'Nothing, I can't do anything, I'm only one person,' then it's worth seeing what other people are doing. It takes only one person to influence change in the world. Jesus is one person. Mother Teresa was one person. Bob Geldof is one person. One person can be an inspiration to many others. There are organisations that are devoted to helping the less fortunate.

In your local parish there are probably many organisations that help others. They might include:

- Society of St Vincent de Paul
- Legion of Mary
- Prayer groups

Find out what groups exist in your parish and invite a member from each group along to the Confirmation session to tell you about the group and how they are working towards a better society.

Larger organisations in the community include:

- CAFOD (Catholic Fund for Overseas Development)
- Christian Aid
- Red Cross
- OXFAM
- Salvation Army
- Shelter
- Missionaries of Charity
- Dr Barnardo's Homes
- Royal Commonwealth Society for the Blind
- SPUC

Try to find out more about these and other charitable organisations.

Write to them and ask how they started, what they do, and how ordinary people can help them in their work.

Perhaps someone from these groups could come and talk to you.

You will soon find out that there is much that you can do. The next problem is can you meet Jesus' challenge to actually do something?

Write down the names of six charities.

Charity	Amount you would give
1.	....
2.	....
3.	....
4.	....
5.	....
6.	....
	total £50

Now pretend you have £50 to give away to the above organisations – how would you split the money. Write in the amount by the charity.

Many years ago the pace of life was very slow. Nowadays it's much faster – perhaps too fast for our own good. Life seems to be one experience rapidly followed by another. There's no time to think properly or reflect on the important things of life.

People often say we live in a consumer or throwaway society.

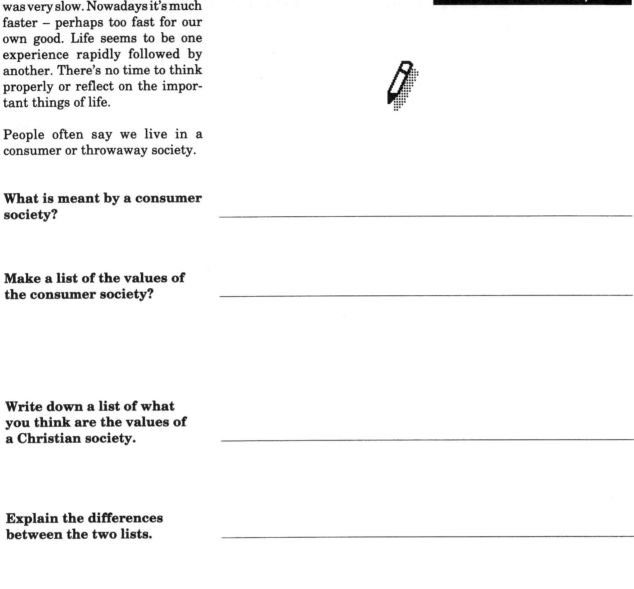

What is meant by a consumer society?

Make a list of the values of the consumer society?

Write down a list of what you think are the values of a Christian society.

Explain the differences between the two lists.

Which do you think is the better society to work towards?

21. The Confirmation Mass

The whole Confirmation Mass is not given here, but only the major parts that differ from a usual Sunday Mass. The particular readings are determined by when the Mass occurs. Examples are given here:

Celebrant: We are gathered together today to celebrate with joy the Sacrament of Confirmation. We pray with our candidates that they and we may be deeply renewed with the love, peace, and joy of the Holy Spirit.

First reading

A reading from Acts of the Apostles (2:1-11)

When Pentecost day came round, the apostles had all met in one room, when suddenly they heard what sounded like a powerful wind from heaven, the noise of which filled the entire house in which they were sitting; and something appeared to them that seemed like tongues of fire; these separated and came to rest on the head of each of them. They were all filled with the Holy Spirit, and began to speak foreign languages as the Spirit gave them the gift of speech. Now there were devout men living in Jerusalem from every nation under heaven, and at this sound they all assembled, each one bewildered to hear these men speaking his own language. They were amazed and astonished. 'Surely' they said 'all these men speaking are Galileans? How does it happen that each of us hears them in his own native language? Parthians, Medes and Elamites; people from Mesopotamia, Judea and Cappadocia, Pontus and Asia, Phrygia and Pamphylia, Egypt and the parts of Libya round Cyrene; as well as visitors from Rome – Jews and proselytes alike – Cretans and Arabs; we hear them preaching in our own language about the marvels of God.'

*** This is the word of the Lord.***

(There is often a second reading)

Renewal of baptismal promises

Priest: We will all stand and join with the candidates as they renew their baptismal promises.

All stand.

Bishop: Do you reject Satan, and all his works, and all his empty promises?

You say: I do.

Bishop: Do you believe in God, the Father Almighty, Creator of heaven and earth?

You say: I do.

Bishop: Do you believe in Jesus Christ, His only Son, our Lord, who was born of the Virgin Mary, was crucified, died, and was buried, rose from the dead and is seated at the right hand of the Father?

You say: I do.

Bishop: Do you believe in the Holy Spirit, the Lord, the Giver of life, who came upon the Apostles at Pentecost and is today given to you sacramentally in Confirmation?

You say: I do.

Bishop: Do you believe in the Holy Catholic Church, the communion of Saints, the forgiveness of sins, the resurrection of the body and life everlasting?

You say: I do.

Bishop: This is our faith. This is the faith of the Church. We are proud to profess it in Christ Jesus, our Lord.

You say: Amen.

All sit except the candidates and sponsors.

Bishop: My dear friends, in baptism God our Father gave the new birth of eternal life to His chosen sons and daughters. Let us pray to our Father to pour out the Holy Spirit to strengthen His sons and daughters with His gifts and anoint them to be more like Christ the Son of God.

The Bishop and priests extend their hands. Each sponsor places a hand on the candidate's shoulder.

Bishop: All powerful God, Father of our Lord Jesus Christ, by water and the Holy Spirit you freed your sons and daughters from sin and gave them new life. Send your Holy Spirit on them to be their helper and guide. Give them the Spirit of wisdom and understanding, the Spirit of right judgment and courage, the Spirit of knowledge and reverence. Fill them with the Spirit of wonder and awe in your presence. We ask this through Christ our Lord.

You say: Amen.

All sit.

The laying on of hands

Bishop: I invite those who wish to be confirmed to come forward.

Each candidate with their sponsor is invited in turn to come forward by the catechists. The sponsor puts his/her right hand on the candidate's (right) shoulder.
The Bishop dips his right thumb in the chrism and makes the sign of the Cross on the forehead of the one to be confirmed, as he says:

Bishop: N......... be sealed with the gift of the Holy Spirit.

You say: Amen.

Bishop: Peace be with you.

You say: And also with you.

Anointing with chrism

1. Lord, on this day of our Confirmation, we pray that we will always be guided by the Holy Spirit to live as responsible Christians, and to use the gifts of the Holy Spirit to good effect.

Lord hear us.

2. Lord, we pray for peace on Earth. Help bring all adults to trust each other, to bring an end to war and conflict, and to work towards the common good for all humanity. Only in this way can adults be a good example for the young to follow.

Lord hear us.

3. Lord, we pray for our planet Earth. May all peoples learn to respect your wonderful creation, and not to leave a spoilt atmosphere, ruined land and polluted waters for the future generations of young people to inherit.

Lord hear us.

Prayer of the faithful

4. Lord, on this day of our Confirmation, we remember all the young people less fortunate than ourselves. The young children who are going to suffer starvation, persecution, incurable illness or abuse. We commend them all to the care of Our Lady, by saying the Hail Mary. Hail Mary, full of grace....

Offertory procession

Along with the bread and wine, take up the project on your saint's name.

22. Let's Party – Celebrations

You probably thought this part was about all night raves. This is actually about another sort of party involving the whole parish. Your Confirmation sessions take place in a small group that involves only the other candidates and catechist. However, your Confirmation is very important for the life of the parish. During the programme you may be asked to take part in two celebrations which involve the rest of the parish. Both celebrations take place during the Mass on two separate occasions. The first is the Celebration of Intention. This informs the parish that the Confirmation programme has started, introduces you and asks the parish for its support in prayer and example. The Celebration of Acceptance occurs at a later date and reminds the parish of the programme and shows your commitment to the preparation for Confirmation.

Celebration of Intention

Sit with your family wherever they wish in the congregation.

Priest: Today, it is the privilege of our Christian community to welcome the candidates who have indicated their wish to receive the Sacrament of Confirmation. I would like to introduce these young people to you. As I read out the names could the candidates please stand.

(The priest reads out the names and you stand when your name is called out)

The candidates are not alone for they have come with their parents, family and friends, whom I also ask to stand.

(Parents and friends stand)

Parents, a number of years ago when your children were baptised, you accepted the responsibility of bringing them up in the Catholic faith. They are being prepared to understand the commitment they are about to take on. I now ask each of you, 'Do you pledge to support your child in the Confirmation programme by encouragement, involvement and prayer?'

Parents: I do. *(Parents and friends sit down)*

Priest: The candidates and their families need all our support and so I invite you all to join me in praying for them at this important stage in their lives. *(Quiet prayer)*

Heavenly Father, we ask you to look upon these young people. May they always be guided by your Holy Spirit, that they may grow in knowledge and love of you. Grant this through Christ our Lord.

People: Amen.

Priest: Shaking hands has always been used in the Church as an important symbol of giving and receiving of peace. It is also a sign of welcoming, of friendliness and of unity. In this spirit, and on behalf of all the members of our parish community, I now shake the hands of our candidates, assuring them of our support and prayers in the preparation to receive the Sacrament of Confirmation.

(Priest shakes candidates' hands)

Celebration of Acceptance

Priest: Our Confirmation candidates have been on the preparation programme for a number of weeks now. Each has decided freely to continue with the programme. To mark their wonderful decision we are going to perform a short celebration using the sign of light.

Light is often used to represent the light of God in our lives. Without God we live in darkness with God we live in light. In Baptism the candidates' parents and godparents were given a candle as a symbol of carrying the light for their children. In honour of this I invite one parent of each child to come forward and receive a lighted candle.

(One of your parents comes forward and receives a candle lit by the priest from the Paschal candle)

Priest: Parents, take the light back to your child and hold the candle together.
Parents, at your son/daughter's Baptism you agreed to carry the light of Christ for your child.

At Confirmation he/she will carry the light for him or herself. As a sign of the increased responsibility your child is to take on, let go of the candle.

Candidates, you are holding a symbol of the light of Christ for yourself. At your Confirmation you will become responsible for your own religious life. May you always carry the light of Christ in your life and be a shining example to others.

(Put out the candle)